KING & QUEEN OF OSE MOUNTAIN

Our Labor of Love

Duane Arthur Ose

KING AND QUEEN OF OSE MOUNTAIN

Stratton Press Publishing
831 N Tatnall Street Suite M #188,
Wilmington, DE 19801
www.stratton-press.com
1-888-323-7009

ISBN (Paperback): 978-1-64895-858-8
ISBN (Hardback): 978-1-64895-859-5
ISBN (Ebook): 979-8-88764-004-4

Printed in the United States of America

CONTENTS

PROLOGUE

Like all stories, there is a before the beginning. Summer of 1982 I was fortunate to explore Alaska. Here are some of the facts you might like to know about Alaska.

1. Alaska has four time zones but uses only one for convenience.
2. Less than 1 percent of the land is owned by the state.
3. Alaska is where men are men and so are the women.
4. Alaska has many temperate zones.
5. The last federal homesteader in America is Duane A. Ose and on the Federal Lake Minchumina Land Settlement Area in Alaska, October of 1986.

The Federal Homestead Act was first opened in 1862 and signed by the then President Abraham Lincoln. A second cousin of mine, Mike E. Ose, drove down from his home in Wasilla, Alaska, to Minnesota to visit. Mike then asked me to ride along with him back to Alaska, and at the end of summer, he would buy an airline ticket for me to fly back to Minnesota. At the two border crossings, Mike told me to have the honor of driving across them. Before the Alaska crossing while at a pullout before the border, I said to Mike, "What's the big woopy deal about me driving across a border?"

Mike sheepishly replied, "I do not have a driver's license."

Apparently, Mike had a driver friend for the drive to Minnesota. Mike was a great host and drove me to a lot of places. I soon realized the rush of traffic was the same as every other state. But I yearned for the far off the grid land. So he began dropping me off at the edges of remote lands where I camped, hiked, and climbed mountains, where seldom people were and were only looked at from afar. One day, I was told that the Federal Homestead Act of 1862 had reopened December of 1982 just for two land settlement areas in Alaska; each were an area of 30,000 acres: the Lake Minchumina Federal Land Settlement, located north of Denali Mountain and about thirty miles northeast of the largest interior lake, Lake Minchumina. The other was the Solana District of 30,000 acres to the southeast by the town of Tok, near the border of Canada.

There are two FBL management offices in Alaska. One in Fairbanks, the other in Anchorage. Mike and went and visited the nearest one, the BLM Office in Anchorage. There I studied the pictures and all the surrounding land or terrain of each.

The Solana District was too close to a main highway, and to get there, I would have to cross native corporation land; it would be likened to trespassing. The timber was good and the lakes very attractive and inviting, but no hills to get above the cold or have solid soil in which to have a good garden or a view, only trees blocking any long-distance views. Lake Minchumina land settlement area was the remotest, high-ground, timber views of the Alaskan Mountain Range, five lakes, solid ground, no permafrost save for down by the glacial tundra ponds, six hundred feet below the hills that really caught my eye. I knew that living up high would mean good drainage and a warm climate. Also, the top of one hill looked like it could be made into an airfield; that would mean easier access to my future home, rather than being on boggy ground and swamp lands.

Already there were sixty-seven people that had filed; most filed on the shores of the tundra's shallow muddy ponds. I picked up an application to file and the rules of what is called Proving Up in order to be approved and become owner of the claim. I also purchased a black and white spy satellite photograph that was taken from space, for $40.

To continue reading the time gap that leads up to the book, *The King and Queen of Ose Mountain,* I would like you to visit books on amazon.com and by looking under my name, Duane Arthur Ose. Order my books of my adventures in Alaska, plus, as of this writing yet to be published before this book, *Rena's Cookbook* and

Marriage of the Heart. Those books lead to the present book. All the books not pertaining to Alaska, you might like as well. I thank you. Now without further ado, I present, *The King and Queen of Ose Mountain*.

CHAPTER 1

Hunt for the Perfect Match Begins

Thank you, Carol Le. You can read about Carol Le in the book *Marriage of the Heart* written by me. Days before Carol died of cancer, she made me promise to keep loving. To search for another to share life with and never be alone. God bless you, Carol Le.

My heart's home is on Ose Mountain, Alaska, 145 air miles southwest of Fairbanks, Alaska. My federal homestead claim is only reachable by a bush plane. Besides that, my proving-up dwelling was one of the requirements in proving up to own, which in my case was a small 9 × 11 foot dugout that a young man, at age nineteen, Jeff Peterson and I made in 1986, read about this dugout in the book, *Alaskan Adventure 2* and the other books that lead up to this one on amazonbooks.com. Search for the name of the author, Duane Arthur Ose.

Where would I find another woman that loved me as well as living on Ose Mountain? Carol Le had viewed all my self-documentation VHS tapes and loved them. Would another woman viewing those tapes help as well? Where to meet that woman? Bars, church, gatherings, by happenstance, it looked hopeless. Mind you, this was the age before dating online. But while paying for gasoline one

Saturday—no, it was not the girl behind the till. You see, while in the checkout line, I browsed the magazine rack. Then along with the gasoline, I bought a big eye caching magazine, *Glob*. To my surprise, the last two pages was a mail order dating service. One page men placed ads, the other page the women placed theirs. No photos, phone numbers, or addresses. The magazine made money by charging for each letter, not the word count of the person's ads. I never placed an ad but only read the women ads. The *Glob Magazine* was the go-between, meaning that if an ad caught my interest, I would mail at a price to the *Glob* for the magazine to send my hello letter or letters on to the person, as it was cheaper to send to six women at a time. The magazine came out once a week, so each week, I sent in six letters and waited. In time after, thirty women were replying. I stopped checking the ads. Most women were not my cup of tea. Or was I to them. Most were looking for rich guys or a fling. It was easy to eliminate most by first reading their ads. I narrowed the thirty down that had favored replying to me to three. Two were living in Canada, one was living in the Philippines. I got a passport and readied for travel to spend a week with each as per agreement among us. There were a lot of phone calls and tons of letters. All three had received copies of my documentary VHS tapes. And none were deterred, albeit, there is nothing like boots on the ground.

The ad that caught my eye was the shortest and right to the point. It read: "Like the cold, cannot stand the heat. Want Northwest Territories or Alaska." My first thought was that this woman knew how to save money and live within her means. Her name was Rena A. A. and was living in Hamilton, Canada. In my days, the kitchens are where the only phone was. I was divorced and Dad had died, so I was living with Mom when I was not in Alaska. I mention the phone because when being called or making calls, Mom from the next room could hear me talk if I did not stretch the twelve-foot coiled wall mounted phone cord outside through the kitchen door. Mom would become all giddy after my long visits on the phone with the three and kid me some. To which were back then long-distance phone calls and cost more than the local phone calls. Mom never charged me for those calls. Thank you, Mom.

Why, you know that I am so old here in 2021 that I remember when we did not have a phone and to call anyone, we had to go to a neighbor's house. That was a mile walk uphill both ways, just kidding, and use their hand crank, one that was high on a wall. A long fast crank would be a long ring and a short crank would be a short ring. Like Morse code. Everyone had a distinct set of longs and shorts. And everyone on the same line would hear the rings. Before cranking a ring, we had to first pick up the earphone to find out if the phone line was in use. The old big wall hanger phone was so high that I had to stand on a chair. Mostly adults used the phones and not often. Then when using the phone, one had to hold a porcelain cup-like thing to an ear while talking loudly into a metal funnel adjustable mouthpiece. Plus, those that had phones would be listening in on your call as well and, at times, join in on the conversation. Like Facebook does now.

Now to continue with *The King and Queen of Ose Mountain*. Then one morning, I was all dressed up with a dress hat and trench coat.

Mom asked, "Where are you going?"

I said, "On a hunting trip."

Mom smiled and kissed me goodbye. I told her I would be back in three or four weeks and that I would call her by and by. With sufficient cash, a brand-new 1990 Nissan pickup bought in full for $8,000, with an added-on topper that I already had, a two-wheel trailer, my packed bag, and headed out the driveway. Made a right turn, drove one and a half miles, and turned north to Ontario, Canada. Leaving the Ose Farm that is located five miles north of the small town of Echo, Minnesota, USA. I was headed toward Ontario, Canada, because that's where my first two women were living. The first in route would be Carlota, who lived in Toronto. The second Rena, living in Hamilton sixty miles north of Toronto. The appointed dates were set for each approximately give or take a day, as I did not know how long it would take me to drive that distance. But what they did not know was that I had planned to be at each of their places a day early to surprise them. We all agreed that I would spend a week each at their apartment.

I am a country boy, not a city boy, thus I am not familiar with getting around, using only an address I like to go by landmarks. Like at that big tree on your right with the red barn on your left, it is than the next place down the road. The house roof is green. It was late in the day when I located Carlota's high-rise apartment building. That was two days before I was expected to be knocking on her apartment's door. I parked nearby on a side street, ate, and people watched, especially the main lobby door of the apartment building. It was like staking out a crime scene. Being it was late, I slept in the seat of the pickup. It was a long night to be sure. After daylight, I bided my time and did some more people watching. After breakfast and at a decent hour with my suitcase, I approached the high-rise lobby's door. Dressed well, walked in, and to my right front saw the main elevator where I was politely greeted by an elevator bellhop that was in a uniform, with a round flat hat with a chin strap. I never had seen a bellhop before but only in the movies. The gentleman bellhop opened the elevator's door without asking who I was. It was like he thought I belonged there and asked me, "What floor, sir?"

I told him. I think it was 19, but whatever, it moved up like it was a two-stage rocket, making me feel heavy, then light as we speed upward. The elevator speeds up and did not stop until I was on the correct floor. Not ever being there before, I looked at the apartment numbers to see which way to go. Carlota's apartment was way down the hall at the end, on the facing end wall. The apartment door had a door clapper and a one-way glass viewing peephole. Mind I was not expected until the next day. I raised the door clapper, let it fall, and stood back so Carlota could see me standing there. I heard her approaching, then still as she must be viewing me. I could then hear the chain latch removed, then the door lock releasing, and then the door swung open. That might be norm for you, but it was a tense few moments for me.

"Duane?" Carlota says.

"Yes. I apologize for being a day early."

"No, that is fine, come in, let me take your coat and hat. I will put your bag in your bedroom."

We then hug and I tell her, "Carlota, you are beautiful."

She, in kind, complements me. I walk into her spacious apartment, and I am amazed at the furnishings and the arrangements. Everything had a place and no clutter. Clean and neat. And no dishes in the sink. The views from her windows overlooked the whole city. Carlota was a beautiful woman of Asian descent. But all Canadian for sure. Carlota almost right away asked me if it was all right to phone her close friends.

I said, "Sure, I would enjoy meeting them."

It was yet early in the day, so a brother and sister friends of hers was invited to come and visit. Soon they arrived, we were introduced, then Carlota said, "Let's us all go for a ride and show Duane the city of Toronto."

We then walked to the elevator and punched the button that said Basement Garage. It was an express elevator, and going down was like free falling. My feet were light, and I felt like I was floating. Soon, the elevator began to slow, as not to have us press to its floor. Then to a full stop. Now we were in the basement garage with countless new shiny cars. They all looked nice. In a short walk, we came alongside a red low sports car, a sports car that I had not seen before. The car's stop light was one whole width of the rear. I thought, *Wow*! But when Carlota stopped over and took her car keys to open it, I said, "Nice car you have."

Carlota said, "It gets me to where I want to go."

The young man and I got in first, tilted the front seat, and wiggled into the back seat. Carlota and her girlfriend sat in front or should I say laid. The sports car had bucket seats, but the occupants were almost in the prone position in them. The visiting was general small talk. Carlota drove out of town, explaining that she loved the country and that we were going to see friends on a horse ranch. The city disappeared; the tar roads disappeared. Grass lands appeared; wood rail fencing began to appear everywhere. Then horses, ranch homes, and horse barns. Then way out in a distance to our right was a big mansion and a horse barn. Not much for trees though, just range land, all flat ground. Ahead on the right was a wide gravel road, a quarter mile long driveway that led up to a big red house. Over the entrance of this driveway was a high arch with the name of the ranch.

Off to either side of the driveway abutted the wood rail horse fence. Between the fence and on the driveway was a level to the drive cattle crossing, that which a vehicle could drive on and over but no horse or cows would for fear of breaking a leg.

When we crossed, I could see a sensor on either side, that would at the house trigger a buzzer, letting the residents know that someone was driving on their driveway and approaching. In driving up this well-maintained drive, I did not see any yard machinery or tractors or anything but the house and horse barn. That is a lot different than what I have seen in Minnesota. Most working farms are cluttered, and machinery is not shedded but left parked wherever, save for access. Even when there are buildings to store the machinery, I could see pride lived here. Part of the open yard drive went past the house on to the horse barn or should I say the stables. To the right appeared to be the guest parking lot. Not all that spread out, but say about 60 feet × 200. The smooth, well-maintained lot also had concrete curbs. Not only that, but near the curb out of the way from a car bumper were one-horse hitching posts and water troughs for the horses. Not just plain posts but metal ones with a small horse head and rings in the noses. There was no shrubbery, only well-cut grass. To the house's entry was a wide concrete white sidewalk. The house was a menace, I would say sixty feet square and built of red brick in decorative art construction. Two and a half stories high, with oval-like, huge, colored, church-style windows. The roof was of clay tile. Moving on to the entry door. It was a huge ornate wood and iron-clad door. The door looked like something out of a storybook. As we approached, the door swung wide open by a butler in uniform. He greeted each of us by name, then said, looking at me, "We have been looking forward to meeting you, Mr. Ose. Carlota has told us so much about you. Is it true that you carry the red lantern for being the last federal homesteader in America?"

"Yes, I am. Carlota is a wonderful lady," I said.

We entered a room of fair size where shoes, coats, hats, any gear was stored. Also, a washroom and I would call it a mud room of sorts. After that, we come into the huge main room. Carlota and the others went on in to visit, while I stood in awe! This room was spacious, to say the least. No less than forty by forty feet. Marble polished floor with decorative designs on it. To my left on the wall side, starting near the door, a wide wraparound marble stairway that led up some twenty-five feet, what appeared to be the cooking and kitchen area. To where I saw two housemaids, Carlota and her friends chatting with the wife. The man of the house was not home. There were no benches or soft sofas, only a long oval conference table, old-style fancy chairs. No TV. No clutter, no stands. One or two green potted plants. From the high ceiling hung a wagon wheel in size fancy chandelier for the main lighting. Otherwise, no floor lamps. There was a dumbwaiter to lower or bring up the food and dishes. But the ceiling was so high, there had to be no space between it and the clay tile roof, save for the insulated roof. A whisper could be heard in that room. We had a lunch with pie at the table, then said our goodbyes and left back to Carlota's apartment. From there, her friends left. Carlota and I visited on, and then I said, "Let me buy us a dinner out."

"Thank you," Carlota said, "But I have plans to prepare our meals here, I like to cook."

That was a plus. Her living room was open to her cooking area. She got right to work, putting on her short white apron over her short skirt. The table was set, the lights were low, and candles were aglow on the table. I was impressed and told her so. Do not ask me what it was that she made, but all her cooking was superb. We ate all our suppers here. Indeed, she loved cooking. No supper club had anything on her as for a romantic place to dine. She had a TV, but it was never turned on while I was there, only a radio playing on a good music station down low for mood music.

In the evenings, we sat on the couch talking, and she had her photo albums to show me and her art hobbies craft work. Carlota was full of questions about Alaska and about Ose Mountain, of how it came to be and looked ahead of what it might look like in the years ahead. Carlota loves my stories of the bear and my other animal friends. She was not one bit concerned about living so far removed from the road. I had the feeling I was talking with a pioneer lady. So far, she had my vote. I sensed the feeling was mutual. From looking out over the city in two directions at this late hour, high above most of it with the city lights and all the lighting each building had, was beautiful. I could tell what office buildings versus apartment buildings by the timing of the lights going off. I had never seen that before. For the seven nights, it was like that. Before we kissed good night, Carlota turned down my bed covers. We said to each other good night. That was when we first kissed. Carlota told me we were going to tour the Toronto Space Needle tomorrow.

CHAPTER 2

Day Two
The Space Needle Tour

"Wakey-wakey, Duane, breakfast is ready. I made us nice fluffy pancakes. In one of your letters, you told me about how and why you come to use brown sugar instead of syrup. I have both on the table. I know sugar is fattening, but it sounds good, so I will try some. I can see why you liked it because it has molasses in it. But to eat five palter-size pancakes with a thick covering of brown sugar on each one, you had to work hard all day every day to keep from becoming fat. You said that after that year, you had even slimmed down to a 36″ waist, wow!"

Yes, I did. Those five loaded sugar pancakes lasted me from 9 a.m. to 9 p.m. But to be sure, I was working hard. At 9 p.m., I ate half a stew pot of a spicy hot dish. Those were the months that I was alone, err, not quite alone, God was with me. As I had told you in a letter, I had run out of syrup but had twenty-five pounds of brown sugar and thought, *Thank you, Lord!*

Carlota said, "When you are out there and six months away from a plane of supplies, you must plan far ahead on supplies. Umm! You were right, Duane, good thinking."

"Well, Carlota, I think out there in the wilderness, God is closer and he is here too, but out there, I seemed to be in closer contact."

Carlota said, "You get ready to see the Space Needle while I wash dishes. I never leave dirty dishes set for even a little while. It is a habit."

"Carlota," I said, "You have only good habits."

Carlota locked the door, and we went to the elevator for another fast-dropping down flight to the garage below. I said, "I might get used to this yet."

Carlota then said, "That is nothing compared to what you will experience on the top of the space needle. You will see, Duane."

She parked, we got out, and I looked way, way up at the Space Needle. Looking up at it gave me the willies; what will it be like on top looking down? I thought the elevator was inside the tower but no. What was more surprising was the elevator was of all glass windows and was on the outside wall. We held hands and stepped in. A mechanical voice said, "Stand back, door closing, hang on for a fast bumpy ride."

It was a fast ride but not bumpy. *Ding!* "Welcome to the dining room floor."

We entered the dining room, and Carlota told me to look down. When I did, I hung on to Carlota to protect her from falling. You see, the floor was all transparent glass. It took me some getting used to that feeling—no, not Carlota—but walking on a glass floor and seeing little cars and dots for the people on the streets below. On the outside up, there were men washing the windows just in harness and nonchalantly cleaning the glass. We had a small lunch at a glass table and watched the people below. Then Carlota asked me if I ever thought of going to the moon.

"No," I said.

"Would you like to?"

"What do you mean?" I asked.

"Above us is a space rocket getting ready for launch that has room for two people. Let us go," she said.

We headed for a second elevator where the sign said, "Trips to the moon this way."

Up we went. A fee had to be paid and a release form signed. Our names were recorded. The pilot was Captain Ose, and the copilot was Carlota. We were about to experience what astronauts experience. Hang on to your seats, readers.

First, we entered the clean room after we were fitted in a clean suit with booties and a head cover. Then men helped us put on our airtight space suits, big boots, oxygen tubes, and a built-in headset to communicate between us and the ground control. The last part was to put on the big round fishbowl on our heads and twist and lock them tight. The men helping us were wearing clean suits and a breathing apparatus. All precautions were so that while on the moon's surface, we carried no germs or contaminants from planet earth. We were now looking at the space capsule. The door was oval with a safe like captain's wheel lock that was airtight and secure.

Carlota was first helped in and seated to the left side of my seat. She was then strapped in. Then me. Before exiting, they gave us a thumbs-up sign, and in return, so did we. On my side was a huge thick round window, the instrument panel ahead of us lit up like a Christmas tree, all green lights and toggle switches. Reachable by each of us. Then we heard "Mic check" in our headsets.

"This is ground control. Captain Ose! Copilot Carlota! How do you read?"

We both said, "Five by five."

Then we were asked, "Are the lights on the panel green?"

I said, "Yes, all lights are green."

"That is confirmed from ground control too. Stand by for engine ignition. 10-9-8-7-6-5-4-3-2-1. Ignition start sequence has begun. Ground control, we have ignition."

Carlota and I feel and hear the rumbling roar of the rockets we are sitting on. Ground control tells us the clamps that hold the ship fast are now released. Then I am asked, "Captain Ose, are all the lights green?"

"Yes," I confirm.

"Copilot Carlota, do you confirm?"

She too says, "I confirm."

Ground control comes on and tells us the launching arm is released. The engines become louder, and our seats are shaking. We get the word. You are a go for launch.

"Godspeed, Carlota and Ose."

We look out the window and see gas and smoke. We are pressed into our seats; G forces are building. In a few moments, we watch the earth becoming smaller.

"Captain Ose, prepare for the booster's separation, on my count, 5-4-3-2-1. Boosters have separated. Captain Ose, you are ready for roll. On my count. 5-4-3-2-1, roll."

We hear people cheering from ground control.

"Captain Ose, prepare for main engine start, on my count, 5-4-3-2-1. Main engine has started."

At that point, we feel even more G force pressing us even more. A few moments pass. Then ground controls comes on and speaks, "Captain Ose, you are a go for orbit."

Looking out the window, we see the planet earth revolving as we are now in orbit about it. The earth may be rotating, but it us that is moving fast around it. Aah, inspiring to see earth from space.

Ground control says, "Captain Ose, prepare to leave orbit about earth and ready for the course to the moon…Captain Ose, we have an emergency. Nothing to worry about, but we are heading you to a splash-down point in the Pacific Ocean. An aircraft carrier is heading there now. Ground control has full control of your destination splash-down point. Okay, we have you on glide path and now are turning off your engine. You are now descending for reentry. It's going to get a little warm on descent, but the heat shield will absorb the heat. Keeping the craft from burning up. You now are over the splash-down point. There will be a few minutes of no communication during reentry. Not to worry. During that reentry, you will see a flame, that is normal. Bits of the heat shield burn off. Not to worry…"

Carlota complains of how warm it is. We feel a jerk as the parachutes deploys. Then we are told to not to worry upon splash down, the craft will momentarily submerge but pop up and float. Boats are on their way to pick you up. We hit hard and see water only, then we go up and bob about on the surface like a bobber. We wait and the bobbing stops. There's a clanking on the hatch door.

The small captain's wheel on the inside is being turned to open the hatch from outside.

I ask, "What gives? Why did we reenter?"

The two men laugh and say, "Well, you see the ground control forgot to put on board the food for your trip."

That was so real, and we never went anywhere. It was all special effects. The G force, the engines, earth seen out the window, splash down, ground control, everything.

"Carlota, that was one memorable trip that I will never forget."

"Well, country boy, we have a trip to make yet, that is back to my apartment," she giggles with a grin.

CHAPTER 3

The Big Question

No, not that question.

That evening, after Carlota's friends had left, I had a very big question to ask. It was gnawing on my mind a long time now. Finally, I couldn't stand it any longer. So I just came right out and asked, "Carlota, how can you afford all this? I mean, the fancy car. High-rise apartment. The lifestyle, your friends. How can you afford this?"

Carlota then said, "You see, my daddy is the president of the Toronto National Bank, and he wants to meet with you tomorrow in his office."

"How much does he know of me?" I asked.

Carlota says, "He has viewed all your documentary VHS tapes, and I have shared all that I know of you. Daddy knows how I love country life and is supportive in every aspect."

It was another nice quite evening and dinner by candlelight with an exchange of long talks about everything. Up high from the streets after hours, the lights were aglow. Like clockwork, one could tell by the tall buildings which were offices and which were apartments by the timing of the lights being on or off. As a country boy, that was noticeable occurrence.

I venture to say Carlota's apartment lights were the last to be turned off. Save for the candle lights.

Good nights were said, and I looked forward to meeting Carlotta's father. Carlota had only good things to say about him. That put me at ease, and I slept well.

"Good morning, mountain man. Breakfast is almost ready."

After a breakfast of a hearty full plate of French toast, we headed to the elevator. Zoom down to the basement car garage to where Carlota's chariot awaited us.

Carlota had a lead foot. And that sports car was used to zoom. I swear that car and she worked together as one. Her car works like they were welded together. Mind to machine.

Wow! I could now see the tall building. I explained, "That is the Toronto National Bank?"

Carlota says, "Not all of it, but it is the largest banking institution around and holds several high finance offices, meaning high rents for the banks building space."

"Look way up there," Carlota says. "My daddy's office is way up on top. We will be going in on the ground floor and wait to be called."

Carlota parks in a space reserved just for her car.

Hand in hand, we walk inside. When we enter, someone greets us.

"Hello," looking at me, the woman says, "You must be Mr. Ose that we all have heard so much about."

I say in turn, "Yes, and hello to you as well."

From the many cubicles and tellers' windows, people raise their heads and look in our direction. Many of them signify hello. Carlota smiles and says hello back.

"Mr. Ose. Carlota. Please have a seat. Your dad will be with you in a moment. He is in a business meeting and will call you when he is ready. He's been expecting you."

The lobby is a menace, but the lines to the tellers are very short. Customers are coming and going with no delay. Cubicles of loan officers are busy with clients.

As I look around, I see tight security with plainclothes men. So nobody's going to rob this place. Aside from that, there is a greeter at the door with a table, coffee, and snacks.

The lounge area is comfortable and not too many people there waiting. Just Carlota and me.

Soon, we are approached by a young woman, saying, "Sorry to keep you waiting, but your dad is ready to see you now. Our elevator man is waiting and will take you up to your dad's conference room where the eleven board of directors and your dad are waiting. Carlota, your father wants to introduce you and Mr. Ose, the last federal homesteader in America and claimed his land in part of one of two 30,000-acre federal land settlements in Alaska. The board of directors and the president, your father, may have some questions to ask of you."

The elevator begins to slow, then speeds up faster, and then slows down. A doorman lets us out and leads us to another big door called the conference room. The elevator man knocks twice and then opens the door and Carlota is first. Everyone stands up, paying their respect to Carlota and then to me.

"Hello, Daddy and all of you, this is Duane Ose."

They all bow their heads to us. Her father introduces each member of the board one by one. Most had French names. Her father pronounced my last name correctly, so right off, I knew he had done his homework.

Pardon me for a side note below.

Ose is pronounced OC. My name originated in Norway. So along with now being referred to as mountain man, I come from a long line of Vikings. You may have heard of the Ose farm in Norway. My four times great-grandfather's name was Oscar Velle, but at that time in history, when one buys property, the buyer also buys the name. To this day, some retain both names and are Ose-Velle. Oscar's one black-and-white photograph of him sitting on a wooden high back chair in a studio at that time was professionally done. The most striking features were his knee-length white socks, bloused in his knee-length trousers with a ribbon bowtie, and his low shoes with leather tongues that had wide, square, large buckles. Now he was a Viking farmer who also knew how to sail a ship. The spelling is Norwegian.

Now to continue:

The board of directors remain standing while Carlota and I walk to the far end of the long oval conference table opposite of Carlota's father, where two chairs await us. I first seat Carlota, then myself. Then everyone sits down.

Then several questions are asked of us, mostly of me and what it involved to homestead. Then I asked Carlota's father, "Sir, do you know what your daughter maybe getting into?"

"Oh yes. I support her 100 percent. I want her to be happy."

After a while. Carlota kissed her father goodbye. We than left the board room, back to the lobby and to her car.

On the way back to her place, I said, "That went well," and Carlota agreed, saying, "Very well."

The day was young, and she invited her young friends for a drive. Together, we went to another house where Carlota and her girl friend went in to visit a lady friend of theirs. I and the young man remained in the car to wait. While we waited, we talked about Carlota. We both agreed she was a wonderful woman. But I said to the young man, "I am somewhat uncomfortable."

"Why is that?" he asked.

I went on to explain, "Because she has a good life here and I do not think it's right to take her from it. It is just a feeling, is all. Carlota is a wonderful person. Something she and I will have to talk about in time."

The young man understood.

The next morning is when Carlota and I would say goodbye at least for a while.

"I like you and all those that I have meet this week."

Carlota and her friend returned, and later, we said goodbye to them and went back to Carlota's apartment to end our last night together.

CHAPTER 4

Day Seven and Day One at Rena's

Have you ever noticed that time stands still for no one? The night flashed by and morning came. Like the stars, their rotation never stands still nor rewinds. Time marches on. Morning was here, breakfast was served. It was time to say our goodbyes, not knowing if we would ever see each other again. Hold that lingering precious moment ever so gently. Hugs and lingering kisses, but no tears. We both knew the score. It had to be. It's time to depart. Time marches on.

Carlotta escorts me out the door with another lingering kiss, looks deep into my eyes, and asks, "I suppose you're going to see another now."

"Yes, just sixty miles down the road at Hamilton, Rena awaits me to fulfill my promise. We must meet."

Carlota looks up at me, holds me by my coat, and speaks, "Can I still write to you?"

I speak, "Yes, I would like that. Very much. No matter what becomes of us."

I leave Carlotta at her apartment door. I walk toward the elevator, glancing back to see if she is watching. Yes, she is. I wave a goodbye. She throws me a kiss.

At each stage, I keep looking back. At her apartment. At the base of the elevator. In the lobby. Then from the car. Waiting for her to come dashing into my arms. But it does not happen. That is how close we had become. Our feelings are mutual. Our ambitions were true.

I slowly pulled away, still looking for her to come running across the parking lot. Telling me to stop. But it was not to be. I went on. To Hamilton where Rena awaits.

The highway was good, but the town was a jungle of streets and houses. Where to look? You see, I am a country boy. I need direction. Rena had given me her address and directions on how to get to her small apartment. It was about midday when I found her apartment. It was a street or cars that park alternately from one day to the next, one side to the other. I was lucky to park in front of her two flat apartments. A housing district. No high rises here. Just steps up and down to the buildings.

Her apartment was one story. Two apartments wide. Nothing fancy. Just a place to live. I parked right in front of her stairs to the apartment and waited for the people to come home from work. Most were women. No cars. And they were just walking home. On the sidewalk to my left. As each woman walked down the street, I looked and wondered, *Which one would be Rena?*

Her place was at this end of the block. So I had a full view of the block ahead of me. At one point, I noticed a woman crossing the intersection, from my right to my left a block away. I was impressed because this woman was carrying two grocery bags. One in each arm. Walking like a trooper and looked like she knew what she was doing. She crossed the street. She came walking down the sidewalk right toward me. I had no pictures of Rena to identify her. As she approached closer, she began to lean to her left and looked at my license plate. Minnesota license plate. Then stepped off the curb and knocked on my window. My window was closed. And I could hear her say, "Are you Duane Ose?"

"Yes, are you Rena?"

Rena stepped back, and I got out of the pickup. I took her bags of groceries and she spoke, "You're a day early. I wasn't expecting you till tomorrow. I'm lucky I bought groceries today."

Rena was very good looking with an intoxicating charming smile. Slender and fit. Black short hair with glasses. I fell in love with her laughter right off. She was also very witty and a great conversationalist.

We walked up a short ten steps about and proceeded down the hall that separated her apartment on the right from a bachelor on the left. The building was of old construction but very soundly done of wood, what I call a stick structure. Why it was high above the street, I do not know. Perhaps it was the style way back when or might it be to keep above a flood plain during heavy rains?

Rena lived within her means. She was divorced due to him cheating on her and more so raised two boys who were adults now and lived in another part of town. Chuck, the oldest, holds a top line job at McMasters University. (Who was named after Chuck Conners, the Rifleman.) And Johnny, a top-of-the-line swimming-pool man that earns a healthy income. Rena raised them well and became wise like her on how to not spend beyond their means.

Rena unlocked and opened the door. We entered the first bigger room that was the kitchen. To the left far end was her door to her porch outside and where she grew some edible plants. As we entered on the right was a solid wall partways into her apartment. Then past that wall was the main room. That had the table chairs and a coffee table and an end window facing the street. To the right of that main long room were the two bedrooms and bathroom between the two bedrooms.

It was a narrow apartment but well arranged. Clutter free. No dust, not even on top the door frames. (As a former army inspector, that was the area I would first check and would say, I will be back when you are ready for inspection.)

The first bedroom Rena was using it for her costume work, making dresses and men's suits or tailor fitting of the suits. That extra income source kept her busy. Often, Rena would tell me of the women who had come with a pattern way too small and she had to first make the pattern larger.

Rena was a seamstress by trade and had started several sewing companies in town for investors and presently working for one as a lead person. Rena was the top-of-the-line boss seamstress. To be sure, I could go on for hours writing about her work. Her clothing of all kinds had many different labels, but all were manufactured at the same place. Only the labels were changed.

After the bathroom was her room. Modest size, nothing fancy. Small single bed. Rena had the habit of fixing up the bed each morning, right up to her last day. May 14, 2020. God bless you, Rena.

That first evening, Rena made a few calls to let all know that Duane's here.

I soon found out that Rena was an excellent cook, not only that, but she took the time to wash and dry the dishes. Put them away and fix the tablecloth. Even setting back in place the chairs. Never once did she not do that. If someone forgot to place their chair back, she did. Rena ran a picture-perfect house.

Rena was on the phone when there was a knock on the door. She asks, "Would you get that, Duane?"

I did just that. Now vision this. I opened the door. There standing in the frame of the door a big giant of a man, filling up the door frame from top to side to side. Then he announces himself, "Hi, I am, her son."

It was her son Chuck. Slightly intimidated at first, I stepped one step back. His mom says, "Hi, Chuck, come on in."

Chuck, it turns out at one time was a Canadian Marine.

After a short visit explaining he thought to come right over as he would be getting up early. All in all, the visit was good for all of us. Chuck was well pleased, as I too. We said our good nights, and Chuck left.

"Duane!" Rena says. "I do not have a spare bed because of my other bedroom is set up for my sewing room. Would you mind if we make a makeshift narrow bed on top the coffee table?"

"That would be fine," I said. After that was made up, we visited into the night and said our good nights.

Her bedroom was only a few feet away to my side. To my pleasant surprise, the coffee table bed was comfortable and not once did I fell off it.

CHAPTER 5

Rena's Day Two

Good morning kisses were made a ritual that never ended. We kissed each other good night and kissed each other good morning. After Rena fixed the beds, she made breakfast fit for a king and queen.

"Duane! I am taking the day off. In fact, every day off while you are here."

Rena called her boss and said, "Frank I am taking the day off. I will be by to show Duane around and introduce him to you and the workers."

Rena, at present, did not have a car. She had in the past but now walks or uses a bus for everything to get around. We walked down that block and on to a bus stop. The way she came home yesterday. I had never been on a public bus. The bus driver knew her and so did a lot of the passengers. Stops were made, but at each stop, we sat still until we were close to her workplace.

We walked and entered her workplace.

"Rena, you never told me the size of this place. It is not just a shop but a factory. Do you know everyone here?"

"Yes."

We pass by the offices where Frank and I think his name was Benny, her bosses and the owners. Rena explains to me this is a complete factory, "From the material to the freighting department. I have helped start factories like this one. My department sews the parts together, an assembly line. When not sitting sewing, I am a supervisor, trouble shooter, and I fix the fast industrial complex machines. I know every machine. My name is called a lot from the employees and even many times from my bosses who, at times, are dumbfounded. I enjoy my work and sewing or knitting. My hands have to always work."

In Rena, I see confidence and leadership. We would have worked perfectly together in the army. Some of the girls see Rena and come to her with questions. She quickly helps them and are back to work.

"This is the first I heard of factory sewing machines," I tell Rena. Then she told me of a new girl that was into sewing but never on a fast zip-zip sewing machine. This new girl had a difficult time in sewing in the zippers on men's jeans.

"Okay," Rena said to the new girl, "Show me how you do them?"

The girl did as she would on a regular machine, using her hands on either side, guilding the pants and zipper. The machine went zip and the zipper had to be taken off because it was not aligned. Rena saw what she was doing wrong. Rena told her, "There is no time to guild the zipper, but instead aim before you press the paddle, putting the machine on. So like a rifle, you aim well and squeeze the trigger to shoot. Now do it."

The girl did it and exclaimed loudly, "I got it! I got it!" The girl was so happy.

Rena held two nice well-made blue jeans in front of me, then asks me to see the difference. She went on to say, "One is way cheaper. Do you see the difference yet?"

"No," I said.

Then she shows me the labels. "The one is a well-known top of the line. Both came off the same line. The only differences are the labels. Johnny soon learned that. He had to have the best. Then I said go to a different store and look for the same thing. He did and learned. Only the labels were different."

Before we left, Frank had her assist one girl on a machine and remedied the problem. Benny was the office man, the money manager. Frank was the grease that kept the factory going.

Rena wanted us to walk to a special marketplace to eat and pick up a few things to bring home. That we did. But on our walk, there a funny thing happened. To set the scene first, every woman or most have large handbags with everything in it. Now vision Rena and I walking across a busy intersection with people everywhere, cars and busses. We are walking side by side. Rena's carrying her handbag low to her side, opposite of me.

We are like in the center of this major intersection, talking and walking, having a good time, plus paying attention to traffic. When suddenly, Rena turns to point out something to me. (Rena is leaning over me as I write this, and I feel she is saying to me why she turned correcting me. But forgive me, Rena.) She turned fast facing me. Thus, yes, you guessed it. As she turned for all the world to see, her bag struck me high up between my legs, slumping me over and in much pain. We laughed and so did those around us. Rena says, "Yeah, that's right."

We die, but memories never do. Know this, our souls never die. Souls are invisible and are with the living. Energy never dies and are detectable. Read my book, *The Ancient Art of Dowsing*, to know how to detect energy fields. Its okay to speak to them if no one overhears you. To think you have gone over the edge. Books are like memories; talking to God is no crime, so be it with a memory.

That day was fun, but it was not over. We returned to her apartment. Rena made supper, and between phone calls from her many friends, we visited on into the night.

We kissed good night with smiles on our faces.

CHAPTER 6

Rena's Day Three

Good morning kisses were made; ham and eggs and toast with milk. Beds made of course. Table chairs in place, washed and dried dishes put away. Tablecloth on. Why we were ready for the calls and some visiting.

Again, Rena calls Frank in case she is urgently needed, but otherwise tells Frank she will not be in today.

Today, we visit her aunt Betty, a close friend. Chuck's wife and her daughters, of which are Rena's two granddaughters named Becky and Kara. Forgive me if I have this wrong, Kara and Rena. But Rena, days before her open-heart surgery, got to be a great-grandma by Kara's baby. Rena was so happy. Rena is probably trying to correct me here, but you have the gist of things.

Later after working hours, Johnny and a close friend of his, Mark, dropped in. Love you still, Johnny and Chuck. One funny thing Johnny told me about his driving, "One day, I was pulled over for speeding. It was a two hundred dollar fine." Johnny looked at the patrol officer and said, "$200.! It's not like I killed someone!"

Rena went on to tell me of some of her adventures with her cars on icy roads and one funny thing. She and Betty were driving, and Rena was pulled over. Rena asked the officer, "Why did you pull me over?"

He pointed to the sign that read, "One way only."

"But, Officer, I am only going one way!"

The officer laughed and said, "Get out of here."

No traffic ticket issued. Betty, her friend, laughed. That was a '67 Chevy. She spoke highly about her friend who fixed cars and gave her advice on hers. If Rena needed anything done on her car, her friend was first to know.

Oh, for the memories. You know what is next, Rena. We kissed our good nights and turned in. I on the makeshift coffee table, made into a bed, and her in her bedroom.

I was just about to sleep when Rena, in her nightgown, came from her bedroom. With these words: "I can't stand it any longer." With no more words said, Rena joined me, or better said, conjoined us as one. And we kissed again, saying good night.

CHAPTER 7

Rena Day Four

We have kissed good morning, eaten breakfast, dishes are washed, table is clean, chairs are placed. When in the front room by the coffee table, Rena faces me with her back to the window. She approaches me, not even a foot apart. Chest to chest, her hands on her hips, elbows out. Looks me in the eye and asks, "Well, are you going to marry me or not?"

I respond by saying yes.

We embrace, kiss, hold hands, and while holding hands, I ask, "Where is the jewelry store?"

Off we walked a few blocks and looked through a window that had rings. We went inside, and in a short time, Rena selected our rings. They were not fancy or expensive. Rena was happily holding us together tight.

"Let's go to the sewing factory."

She showed some of the girls her ring. That caused some excitement. Then we went to the office where Frank and Benny were.

"Frank!" Rena said. "I am giving you my notice. Duane and I are getting married."

Frank was a gasp and said, "I don't believe it."

Then Rena held out her hand and showed Frank the band of gold.

"Well, I'll be darned," Frank said.

Of course, everyone in the factory was told. Best wishes and lots of hugs were shared as we left, waving our farewell. Rena was so happy.

Rena was busy that day being on the phone, calling her brothers and sisters, her boys, and her many friends. She even told her landlord, and there were no problems there. As she was leaving with me to first Minnesota, then on to Alaska, to Ose Mountain.

Within the next day, day five, we were packed. The pickup topper and the two-wheeler trailer were full, no room to spare. Her boys helped us. It was both a sad time and a happy time. An emotional time for all.

At first dawn's light, day six, we would begin the journey. It was like the federal homesteaders that came to be because of the Federal Homestead Act of 1862, signed by Abe Lincoln. To open the west for settlements. Only in our case, the act had reopened for the last and final time in December of 1982, 120 years later. In time, we would be on Ose Mountain the last Federal Homestead to file on October 12, 1986, in America and in the center of Alaska seventy-seven miles true north of the tallest mountain in the North American continent, Denali Mountain, first called the Great One or Big Bear by the Native Alaskans.

Ose Mountain is not a mountain; in fact it is but 1,405 feet above sea level. But when walking up hill three and a half miles after a tundra pond landing with a full pack, it can then be called a mountain. Just ask Rena.

Ose MTNs airfield is 2,000 feet north of the Log Castle Airfield is 1,300 feet by 150 feet. East to west runway. The airfield was completed in three years by after-hours work time of building the log castle. Google earth map to see the cleared airfield and perhaps the green roof 2,000 feet south and the cleared lawn and garden. Only populated areas have defined close views. Ose Mountain is hard to see but look for the elevation 1405 and the east west runway.

N. 64 degrees 11.684 Min

W.151 degrees 23.739 Min

(Read my previous books on, amazonbooks.com under my name, Duane Arthur Ose, to be brought up to speed on how Ose Mountain came to be.)

CHAPTER 8

Busted at the Border Now What?

With a packed truck and trailer, we headed toward the USA border that was en route to Minnesota from Hamilton, Canada. No big deal. Well, guess what?

We stopped, and the border guard looks first at us. A happy couple. Then at the full truck and full trailer.

"What's this?" he asked.

"Oh, this is all Rena's belongings," I happily say. "We are headed to Minnesota to be married."

The guard looks up to the sky with his hands down to his sides limp and sighs and says to himself, "Oh, this is going to be a long day."

Instantly, two armed guards approach us with fully automatic machine guns. I think they were Ozies. Rena and I were separated. She was directed by one guard to a room, and I was ushered by the other into a second small room.

I was then educated on what procedure it was to get married to a Canadian. The long and the short of it. The paperwork had to be first done and then a six-month waiting period. Rena and I were allowed to leave, make a U-turn, and head back.

Rena was not happy. I said not to worry. We drove back and her two sons met with us. After hours of scratching our heads, Chuck or

Johnny suggested, "Mom, you pack your big steamer trunk and get a day pass to the bus station in America for a day of shopping, which was a daily routine for Canadian shoppers. It would mean that you will have to leave most things behind, and Duane, you can bring a few things of Mom's as not to bring attention. Mom, you stand on a corner of the USA bus station parking lot, and you, Duane, drive there and pick her up."

"Sounds like a plan, thank you. But no way am I going across the same border crossing. They know me there."

The next day, we do that. Rena gets on the bus, and I head for the other border crossing by Niagara Falls. By the way, Rena has the biggest trunk I have ever seen. It was so heavy that Rena could hardly lift it, but she did.

I approach the border checkpoint. Close, now an alarm goes off and lights are flashing. A guard tells me to step out of the pickup and follow him. We enter a small barren room with one chair facing four barren walls. With a window very high for only light to shine in and so high that one could not escape through them. I do not know what is up. I think it was my license plate number that set the alarms off.

Two men were in another room. Most likely checking on my history. But as I looked more around, I spotted little cameras up high trained on me. That's why the chair was fixed in place. I sat still looking calm and relaxed. For what seemed an eternity, thinking of Rena standing on a corner worried about me.

A guard came up to me and asked, "Did you try to cross a border yesterday?"

"Yes. I was educated and know now what must be done to be married to a Canadian. It's about six months and paperwork. I had no idea."

The man then says, "Okay, you are free to go."

As I pull away, I noticed I was not the only one pulling away. Right behind me was an unmarked detective's car. It had black wall tires. A radio antenna on the trunk and two men in the front seat. Coincidence, I do not think so. I drove under the speed zone. Headed for the main highway that would bring me to the big central bus station. Along the way, I pulled into a gas station not for gas, but to see what that car behind me would do. I went inside and back to my pickup hasty-like. To which one man went inside to probably ask the tenant what I may have asked him.

I got on the highway, and that car did too and right close no car length apart. I was coming up on the clover leaf to turn on it, and that car was tight behind. Now vision this. Instead of slowing down for the on ramp, I remained at the maximum speed limit. That car was right on me. The on ramp came and I yanked the steering wheel hard to the right. I was now traveling up the on ramp, and that car could not react in time to follow me.

I had shaken them. Onward, I went to the bus terminal like we planned save for me being late. There on the corner stood Rena. I pulled to the curb to help Rena with her huge trunk. But not talking, she with the back side of her hands down low and with her eyes directed me to notice the car sitting on the side next to me. The back side of her hands were flinging her fingers to move on. It was another unmarked detective car with two detectives.

It was quick sign language with her eyes and hands out of view from the detectives, she indicated to me to pick her up on another corner. I nodded affirmatively and drove away. I gave her time to reach that corner with that big heavy trunk to drag or carry with both hands.

Finally, I loaded her trunk and we drove off. Being alert not to go over the speed limit and be on the lookout for more detectives in the front seat for a long way.

We spoke of the adventure we just had. It was still a long way to the Ose farm to introduce Rena to Mom. But that is another chapter.

CHAPTER 9

Ose Farm to Ose Mountain

The Ose farm is near now. Two hundred acres. It is where I grew up. Located in in the township of Sioux Agency in the county of Yellow Medicine. My church was Rock Valle. I went to a public school in a small town of Echo. Graduated 1960. My worst subject was English, taught by Mrs. Hanson. My best class was science taught by Mr. Roberts. As science club president. A story would be written on when after school one day, I almost blew up the science room by making nitroglycerin.

"We are here, Rena. The house and Mom are down that quarter-mile driveway."

Mom and Rena hit right off, and they were family. They had a lot in common. Mom was a sewer too and made an extra income by doing upholstery. Mom had a shop north side of the house.

Rena and I were married in the Yellow Medicine courthouse on December 14, 1990. Mike, my brother, and his wife, Susie, were our witnesses. Being it was the winter months and was not conducive to move up to Alaska, as there we need to do much before, we could winter. Fortunately, we found a house to rent, and Rena found work at a nursing care center at the Granite Falls Hospital, a twelve-mile drive.

In order to work and not yet a citizen, she had to get a green card in MPLS some 150 miles away. So we did. Rena loved work and I drove her to work and back every day for two reasons. One, she did not know how to drive a 5-speed stick our pickup, and the other, she no longer had a driver's license anyway. Not since she lived in Canada did she drive again.

Springtime came, and we soon would be leaving for Ose Mountain in Alaska. Rena likes cats, so we looked the newspaper ads over every day. Speaking of ads, I took her to where I found her ad in a *Glob* magazine. I will never forget the words she wrote:

"Like the cold, can't stand the heat. Want Northwest Territory or Alaska."

Then one day, Rena showed me an ad. It said, "Found an angora female cat. Free to a good home." Rena said, "I want to see her."

Rena called.

"Yes, we still have her."

"Okay," Rena says, "We will be there to see her."

Forty miles later, Rena and the cat were together and fell in love with each other right off.

"I will take her," Rena says. Rena named her a French name, Me-nun, French for girl cat.

Early June, we loaded up the pickup and made a makeshift wood-raised plywood platform of two-foot sections to remove a section as needed to remove or get to any stored items under the full length assembled platform. We would crawl in to sleep. It was not easy, but it was good enough for us.

There is one hitch. Mikki Ose, a second cousin of Wasilla, Alaska, hears of us moving to Alaska. He flies to Minnesota, buys an old truck, and fills it with antics of all kinds. Potbelly ornate stoves, safe, cash register. The box is full of stuff that is both his and ours; it even has side boards to hold things. With mine towed behind. Mike bought the towbar and gave us cash for gas and expenses.

The cat had to have shots and papers to prove before crossing any boarder. That was fifty dollars. No big deal, but Rena brings it up when we cross into Alaska. Watch for it. It is a funny remark she made.

By now, I had driven the Alaskan Canadian Highway, ALCAN, several times and knew the seasons not to be on it with a two-wheeler truck.

Along the way, we took in the sights and museums, plus Liard Hot Springs and the signpost at Watson Lake, where I have two signs, the town sign of Echo and the Lower Sioux Agency sign. I really like the homemade sign, made of a toilet seat: "Flushing, Michigan." When traveling that highway, stop in to see it and bring a sign. There is an office that is a directory telling you where every sign is and how it all started.

The Alaska border is ahead. Rena readies the papers for Me-nun. We stop to be inspected. I am asked where you are headed.

"Wasilla," I tell him.

"Okay, move on."

Rena said, "Stop. By ——, we paid fifty bucks for Me-nun's papers."

The guard laughs and says, "Okay, you are good to go."

From there, we drive the road left that heads to Anchorage but stopped thirty miles short of that big city to where Mike Ose lived off mile marker 39 on the George Parks Highway. We unload his stuff. Call the pilots up at Nenana to give them a time to expect us. From the float pond there, we are to be flown to the lake I call Levi Lake; from there, we will walk three and a half miles to our dugout.

CHAPTER 10

Loading at the Nenana Float Pond

After Rena insisted that her girl cat Me-nun's papers were checked at the Alaskan border and near the small town of Tok, Alaska. We filled Molly with gasoline and had eaten at a mom-and-pop restaurant there. I kicked the tires and checked the trucks over. Rena, with her water spray bottle, cleaned the wind shield, the side mirrors, headlights, taillights, and side windows. We were about ready. Last but not least, Rena clipped on Me-nun's leash and went for a walk. Then we loaded up and left Tok.

Exiting Tok, there's two choices. Left is to Anchorage, straight ahead is to Fairbanks. Mike lived outside the town of Wasilla, off mile 39 or 39 miles north of Anchorage, on the George Parks Highway. So left we went, toward Sarah P. hometown. I first met her before she was the city mayor of Wasilla. Then later, after she was Alaska's governor. The last time she and I talked was at a Wasilla auto service counter scheduling work to be done on her car. That day we talked was two days before she was chosen to be John McCain's running mate for the President of United States.

Personally, Sarah should have run for president. I would vote for her in a heartbeat. Fine, savvy, smart, thorough lady. I watched her in the debates for Alaska governor. Sarah put the other two stuffed shirted men in their place and won.

At Mike's home, he and I offloaded his antiques. Stayed the night and the next day drove 300 miles north to Nenana with Molly pulling our pickup. Mike later got a friend to drive his truck back. Remember, Mike had his driver's license revoked. Of which that day I was reminded.

Rena and I had a rendezvous time to meet two pilots at the Nenana float pond to fly us and our stuff out that day. The George Parks Highway is a main road in Alaska. A fast road. From Anchorage to Fairbanks is 350 miles. The distance from Mike Ose to Nenana is 260. I know every bump curve and speed zone on it. No problem, right? Wrong.

Past Healy now, the coal mine area not far to go. I was pulled over. I walked back to the highway patrol car and entered his back seat.

"Driver's license please."

(Mind you, every patrol officer in Alaska knew Mike Ose.)

"Duane Ose."

"Do you know Mike Ose?"

"Yes, he is one of my second cousins. The black sheep of the family, but a good guy, he has not killed anyone."

The officer then asks, "Where you headed?"

"Nenana, sir. We are flying to a lake today and the pilots are waiting."

He smiles and tells me slow it down a bit.

"To be sure, Officer, and thank you."

I get back in the pickup and explain to Rena what just happened.

"Wow, you Oses are known all over."

All in all, we are ahead of schedule, so we stop at the Rough Woods Inn, owned and run by Ruth and Larry Coy, good friends, and if you are ever in Nenana, stop there to eat or rent a motel room. Fairbanks is fifty miles more. Food is great and the rooms are reasonable in price and well cared for.

Ruth and Larry were enamored with Rena. Larry, on the side, gives me a thumbs-up. Ruth packs us a lunch before we leave and says, "Here, you guys will need this."

Rena says, "You know I will never forget your kindness."

Later, Rena keeps Ruth supplied with rhubarb that is for pies.

We arrive at the float pond. The pilots know I have a dock to tie up their planes and offload our stuff, having been there several times before. Levi Lake is about 100 air miles SW from Nenana or 145 air miles SW of Fairbanks. At that time, I had a PO box in the Nenana post office. That in the years to follow changed to a post office in Fairbanks.

Nenana is a good village to live in but with one drawback. It is in a flood zone, so basements are not advised and seek the higher ground in that area to live. Nenana is famous for the Nenana Ice Classics. Prize money is paid out to the nearest guess of the time the Try-pod moves. However, many that pick the right time share equally the prize. Winning prize on average is $300,000. Call and buy as many guesses as you can afford or go online. Tickets are $2.50 and has been the same cost since I remember. One time, I missed by four minutes a prize of $300,000. One I know has won four times. He is a nut though, as he is a busy guy checking the ice and records of the times it has gone out. The tickets must be entered by a certain time to qualify. All that information you can get if you buy tickets. Or Google "Nenana Ice Classics."

All Alaskan Villages at the mouth of a river ends in a *Na*. Thus Nenana or Tanana extra.

Rena has never been in a small plane. I instruct her on how to avoid becoming airsick. Morning flights are the smoothest. If you start to become oozy, stop looking out the windows. Focus on a spot inside the plane ahead of you and move with the plane; do not fight it but move with it. As once a pilot, I never got sick because I was one with the plane. For first-timers, fly in the early morning for smooth air. You will read this in the book *Marriage of the Heart* by me.

Rena quickly gets to work, opening the truck loads of stuff. We help the pilots pile in and organize the stuff for balance and so as not to overload as well. Every plane has a weight limit. The planes we are using are small. What cannot be flown out to the lake today will be flown out tomorrow. One thing sure, the bag of Meow Mix is on board. Plus, some gasoline for now. Later in the week, we will have a whole plane load of gasoline flown out to the dock. We have months of bulk food on board. Water will be collected at our spring.

We kiss and climb on board. Rena is in one and I'm in the other.

Rena's plane starts up. *Click-click* and then *pop* and *roar*. Her plane starts moving away from shore and moves to the end of the pond, facing into the wind. I was trained to always use the full length of the runway or, in this case, the float pond.

We wait. The pilot of her plane is warming up and checking the gages. Then her pilot powers up. The sound is deafening; from shore to shore, the wake of the pontoons is widespread. The plane moves faster and faster. Both pontoons or floats are yet in the water. The pilot tips the plane to the left a bit. This move raises the right float out of the water. The plane is moving faster now, and the left float is above the water. The plane now is airborne and rising. We have lift-off. Rena is on her way.

Now it our turn. Soon, we two are up there. For miles, we fly side by side well apart. Then Rena's plane takes the lead. Before we land, the planes fly over Ose Mountain for a look-see. Rena's pilot is showing her where she will be walking and maybe she can make out the dugout.

One by one, we land. Using the whole length of the mile-long lake. Not needing it, but to be safe, we do. The planes skim the water, then *splash, splash*, settles down, and the rudders levered down in the water to steer the planes to the dock like boats. One at a time. I go first to get out and pull the plane tight to the dock. Tie it fast. Unload. Push the empty plane clear, and Rena's plane taxies up and I grab the wing strut and pull the plane to the dock, tying it tight.

Without a dock, we would have to have chest waders to waddle ashore, through wet tall grass and mud. The time and work in building this dock has been well worth it. No way would I live down here with shoreline grasses and two thousand feet deep permafrost to build on.

Rena and Me-nun step out. Rena holds my hand, feeling a bit oozy. Then the stuff is unloaded. The one pilot says, "I will be back with gasoline and the rest tomorrow about this same time."

(Pilots never fly out to Ose MTN empty.) Later, I will be loading the plane with empty gasoline drums when next a plane arrives with a load.

The two pilots wish us well, and Rena and I wave them goodbye as I shove the planes from the dock.

The planes start up. *Click-click*, a shudder and shake, and the engines start. Like two ships, they take to the sea. Headed downwind and turn into the wind. One by one, they power up. Light now, it takes no time, and they are airborne. But the sound is echoing from shore to shore for a time. We watch them fly away. The sound lingers and then all is quiet. We are alone.

CHAPTER 11

Time Out

In order to bring you, the reader, up to this moment where Rena and I are about to begin our walk up to the Ose Mountain dugout. Besides reading my previous books pertaining to Alaska, also read *Marriage of the Heart.*

The last time my boots were on this dock where Rena and I are now was on or about the June 15, 1989, when I, upon reading a letter from Carol Le, was devastated.

(Carol and I were a couple. But this year, she remained in Minnesota.)

The letter read, "Dear Duane. They have found me to have cancer and I only have a few months to live."

I medially rushed to Minnesota to be at Carol's side.

Read about Carol in *Marriage of the Heart.*

The dugout had sat empty from June 1989 to now, mid-June 1991. So imagine what Rena was about to step into.

Rena's dugout home for nine years.

We began our three-and-half-mile hike up to the dugout. Rena in the lead with Me-nun on a leash. I followed with a full pack on my back. The rest of the stuff remained on the dock at the mercy of the black bears, but I had the food stuffs on my back.

Early in the morning, I would be back with my ATV that was stored and its trailer to bring the rest up to the dugout. And again, later in the day, to receive the rest that is being flown to the dock.

At that time, I was still using the Frenchman's cabin as the head courtier's site. The top airfield was yet to build

As we walked, I pointed out the points of interest to Rena.

The Frenchman's cabin, the enchanted forest, a growing sinkhole, rifle ally, moose yard, the golden forest, the ridge, the overlook view to Denali Mountain 77 miles true south, the Alaskan Mountain Range, the five lakes to the south. Then the basement hole of 31×41 for the house to be built. I myself dug this by hand in eleven long twelve-hour days in September 1987.

This was June and the longest day was the twenty-second, so it never got dark, thus enabling us to see.

Over the ridge facing east was the dugout of 11×9 feet that nineteen-year-old Jeff Peterson and I built in 1986. The dugout was built between September 15 and November 11, 1986. It was a habitual dwelling that was approved by the federal government inspector, as per one of the proving up requirements in order to be granted the property. July of 1987, I completed all the requirements and was approved along with having to pay 12.5 cents per acre. The same few they had to pay in 1862 under the Federal Homestead Act of 1862, signed by Abe Lincoln.

"Welcome to your new home, Rena."

This door was a trick door with a secret locking mechanism that could be locked when not home. I got this idea from the Egyptians of long ago.

I first pulled the wood birch burl that was in a board hole over to the side above, out just a bit. This pulled inside the wall frame leather shoestrings (two, in case one broke) that raised and released the locking off center toggle that held the door latch on the inside. Then pulled on the wood door handle to unlatch the door. Held and pulled the fancy tree root handle. Swung open the 4×6 foot vault-like door. The door had two full-width large wood door hinges (18-inch dowels in the hinges). The wood door was a hollow door and insulated with a 3-foot square triple pane Plexiglas window. Seldom was this lock used, but in the time of our absence, gave us great security and peace of mind. No bear could get in and only a man with a chainsaw could gain entry. Besides, it was fun to make.

The roof was made of birch logs with twenty-one mills of back poly sheeting and to cover that was six inches of ground covering green moss and dirt for dryness and warmth. A wood stove to heat, and before Rena, I cooked with wood.

But Rena and I hauled up to Nenana an apartment-size LP range and a washing machine, which will be flown in.

The dugout had an insulated double wall with moss for insulation. Both inner walls and outer walls had vapor barriers. Plus, the wood floor also was vapor barriered. This way, we never had black mold.

In the back wall, we cut and built a door 4×4foot. Then I tunneled a 4×4×9 foot tunnel and encased that too with wood. That was our fridge. Cold hole at +38 degrees year around. Where we stored things like you would in your fridge, save we stored stuff that lasted more than six months at a time.

The dugouts celling was 9.5 feet high. High to hang things like lamps, etc. Space for a table, sitting bench, a rope double bed, LP cook stove, portable clothes washer and dryer.

Every corner had shelves and on all the walls. Gun rack. The bed was high enough to slide under it five-gallon buckets.

We soon called the dugout a two-step cabin. It was only two steps to everything we owned. For heating, it took little to heat perhaps two cords of wood. One cord measures out at 4×4×8 feet.

Later, Rena wanted a window that faced the sun to start plants. That was fun. Sparks flew as I used the chainsaw and cut a window opening. I made the window to swing outward from its bottom with a shelf inside for her plants.

Now let's hear Rena speak into a VHS camcorder. Her letter to her mother the first night in the dugout. To be mailed out tomorrow.

The camera is held close to her face. Rena is all giddy and silly. She holds nothing back.

"Look, Mom. You have one crazy daughter. I have just walked uphill three and a half miles. To a hole in the ground. It is all musty and dirty. No one has lived in here for over a year. Bedding is damp. Stiff cloths are still on the clothesline."

Rena looks at her wristwatch and says, “It is now two in the morning and I am tired.

CHAPTER 12

Early Years of Life in the Dugout

The dugout was easy to heat, easy to cool. Secure from weather and bears. Up high from the bottom land meant warm air versus often freezing cold of -80 below zero. (The coldest we have ever seen in over thirty years in one day was -20 below zero F.)

Soil was fertile and good drainage. Elevation meant good communications. In those years, it was long-range analog for cellular bag phones and TV. I had a big stick citizen band antenna and, under that, an all-channel TV antenna.

In the dugout with our DC seven-inch TV, we were able to watch three TV channels from Anchorage some three hundred miles due south.

For water, we had two sources. One, a hillside pond I had dammed to hold 8,000 gallons of rain and snow melt. That pond was higher than us, so we had gravity feed to our garden sprinklers as needed. That water was also at times used for washing clothes.

The other source was the spring. I had plumbed it to be safe for drinking and easy to fill our water wagon. We never had to boil water or was ever short of having water.

We had a choice of hanging a shower bag in the dugout or outside in a shower house. In the dugout, a shower meant we had to stand in a round metal tub. One time, while it was winter, the wood stove was hot, and I dropped the bar of soap. Instantly, I bent over to pick up the soap and branded the raised name of the cast-iron stove on my buttocks. My butt sizzled like a branding iron to a calf at branding time. Rena laughed and laughed. Never again did she or I drop the bar of soap.

For years, we had the supply plane scheduled to come every six months, bringing not only supplies but mail too.

Rena, before the six-month plane arrived, would prepare the grocery list for the pilot to shop for us. The six months revolved around the springtime and mid-wintertime. Try to imagine writing a list of food and other things six months ahead. Rena's saying if something was forgotten, oh well, we just had to go without.

Sometimes, we would not see anyone for six months, and that would be the pilot.

For the people that did not have two-way communications (us), there was Trapline Chatter located in a small town named the North Pole twelve miles south of Fairbanks. Letters and calls were sent in and saved to read on the radio each night at 9:30 p.m. Rena and I would tune in in case of any letters were for us. It was a free religious public service. Thank you, KIAM Trapline Chatter.

Out there away from civilization and the rush, I for one and Rena too was closer to God. Our church and God were within us. More so than in a church building.

Rena was, shall I say, clairvoyant. Rena told me this one experience that you all must know.

This occurred while I was working outside. She was sitting, sewing or knitting, facing the wall below the rifle rack. In her words. "I looked up at the wall. I saw like a screen. And on the screen. (She goes on to tell me.) Do you remember on a screen watching the rubber ball bouncing from left to right? It was a small twinkling light bouncing across. It suddenly stopped still a moment and jumped off the screen and entered me in my chest or heart. I seemed to know that it was my mom, telling me she is fine." Rena then told me that she (Rena) felt happy and blessed.

Mail time took a few days to get to KIAM. About that night on KIAM, we were read a letter from Rena's family that their mom had gone to heaven. I hugged and held Rena in my arms. But we know now that love has no bounds. Rena's mom had said goodbye, and Mom is fine.

Something like this again happened to Rena; while Rena was asleep, she had a dream. She was walking along a stream and came to see me building a bridge. At one end, two men stood and saw her looking at me. The men said, "Don't worry, Duane knows what he is doing."

Rena describes the men, and I realized the two were my uncles Roland and Milo Bue (who were in heaven). At that time of Rena's dream, we were building the log house.

One early morning, I was yet in bed. Rena went outside and came back in and said there's a porcupine by the dogs. (Porcupines are bad news to dogs.) Resting in bed yet, I pointed to the rifle rack and said, "There's the gun."

Gun in hand, she went out and *bang*. Came in put the rifle back and said, "I got it."

Another time, we were both soon to have supper. Rena looked out the side window and quickly said with a slight stammer, "Ah, we only have two dogs, right?"

I looked and said, "Yes, that third one is a wolf."

Wolves mate with dogs and this one had taken a shine to Mya. Her mom Chena, in dogs' language, talked her daughter out of following the young wolf.

Rena and I went out to watch all this. Mya really wanted to go with the wolf, but her mom made it clear not too.

Now you might want to read my third book, *Alaska Wilderness Adventure 3*, concerning the wild people I came to refer to as the Hairy Ones. I mention this because I told Rena of them.

Rena, at one time, told me she was near one and sensed being watched and of the smell that she smelled. I reassured her that they mean no harm.

We had a garden about 200 × 150 feet, a greenhouse of 16 × 36 feet, 17 rhubarb plants. Rena canned a lot. Rena and the bears went side by side in the berry patches. Rena was there boss. Bears respected her. The biggest black bear named Bear, Rena often would have a bag of homemade popcorn for him when he came by to visit.

On next to our first day working on the log house. Then to get the highlights of *The King and Queen of Ose Mountain*.

CHAPTER 13

The Castle's Foundation Begins

Queen Rena and King Duane begin building on day 2 of settling in the 11×9-foot dugout.

In book 3, read how in 1987, I dug the basement and girdled 140 majestic spruce trees to dry while standing to be ready to fall and treat or preserve when I returned with my Queen Rena.

(Girdling: The way that I do it is. Using a chainsaw and just up from the base of the tree, I make three one-inch-deep cuts at one inch apart. One cut is not enough. The flowing sap of the tree will heal closed, allowing the tree to continue drinking water from its roots. Three cuts are to ensure that healing closed will not occur.)

Then in time, the tree will dry from the top first. The best time to girdle is before spring. Then by fall, the tree is ready to fall and use in the making firewood. Or in this case, I girdled the trees at the end of September of 1987 where they supper dried until June of 1991.

Any wood below ground grade must be treated and made to last an eternity. Even when building in the ground with concrete blocks, the outer surfaces of the blocks need special treatment to keep the wall dry. So many basements are wet and uninhabitable. Thus, half or a third (if tri-level) of the house is a wasted space.

Upon Rena's inspection, she pointed out that the basement excavation needed to be dug back more into the hill. She said we need room in the front of the basement back away from the drop-off view steep hill to safely drive our vehicles, snowmobiles, and ATVs in the drive-in basement. Rena was right.

After I had dug another five feet back, Rena gave me the go ahead to get the logs hauled up for the basement. Like a king and queen, we worked together. But each have their expertise or skills. That way, there is bliss.

You men. When it comes to building a home, include your wife's input.

I dug the basement large enough to fit the outside of the log walls of 30×40 feet. I was careful to keep the grade of the excavation level by using my dad's transit. Also, I never removed in any area deeper. That way, the ground would remain solid.

The basement log walls would be made "peace sir peace style." Posts with V-scribed logs stacked between each post. Posts would be placed every ten feet. The posts would have for the scribe-fitted logs a flat side on two sides, with a mitered 4×4-inch chainsawed miter cut for the mitered ends of the logs to fit and slid down together tight Not nailed but allowed to settle. On the top inside and outside, I secured a board trim with vapor barriers and fiberglass insulation. The wide trim board was made in a wavey design to be decorative appeal and attached to the base of the second story.

After the basement, the real log house is built on the basement posts. In the best way to build with logs. Chink-less. V scribed. Round notch. High ceilings and no nails. The logs float and has withstood an earthquake of 7.2.

I copied the plans from the house named the Kerry Street House in Canada. See and read two books on B. Allen McKey.

Counting the number of 2-0inch diameter × 16-foot posts needed to include the 4 posts in the center of the basement spaced 10 feet apart in a square, totaled 18. Holes would be dug five feet deep exactly. No loose soil left at the buttons. The soil was not earth, but volcanic ash. (Burned stone from a nearby volcanic eruption millions of years ago.) No wood would touch the ash. The dry wood would be first soaked by a copper treatment and then wrapped by 40-pound asphalt felt. No wood any of any part of the house or porches, etc., touched the ash or soil.

Now after squaring driving stakes in where each post was to be. With our ATV and log bob, one by one, hauled up and into the basement. Rena and I peeled each first, then with a wood tall tripod and a 4 to 5 ratio block-and-tackle raised and placed the posts as they were ready.

By the way, Rena peeled over 2,000 logs in building that eminent structure. Mom too flew up twice and helped Rena peel the logs. Once Mom was pulling the bark, I heard her let a real ripping fart. We laughed and laughed. Plus all the lumber was milled on site by a $150 chainsaw attachment. Rena and I worked as a team. Sawing over 2,000 board feet of all sorts of lumber. Also, Rena's kitchen was all made of our birch by Rena and me.

Somewhere at this point, I asked Rena, "Do you have anything to say on the movie camera?"

Now holding a cant hook business end up, hugging it, she smiles and speaks, "Yes. I want to go home." Then says, "Okay, back to work."

While digging one of the four center post holes, we made a discovery like no other. Black bones. I, loving science, stopped the dig. The dig had now become an archaeological site.

The scientist within me went to examine closely.

This is what we found out. First, there had been two eruptions. How did I know this? Because at nine feet down from the surface of that area of the dig, not the hole, there was a thin line of once black soil made from vegetation. Perhaps an eight-inch thick. This hill was a stone hill and covered by two volcanic eruptions; the first was fifteen feet deep. Then a period of vegetation. Followed later by a second eruption, the last one. This one was nine feet, covering the time between the first one.

Now back to the bones. I, by searching and expanding the dig, found more bones on that black line of earth. Here is the picture I formed in my head. The animal had been killed by wild animals and torn apart. Spreading the parts wide and eaten, save for the big bones.

Then *kerboom* the second volcano eruptions ash covered the beasts' shredded parts while the kill was still fresh.

I never did find the skull. The bones were the size of arm bone and wrists. I broke open one short leg bone (could clearly surmise the animal was not a deer, moose, or a reindeer but small in stature) and strangely found it to be empty. No silt where the marrow had dried and was gone.

Thus, my conclusion of the animal's death was just before the eruption. But time for the marrow to have been dried and gone.

Mistakenly, I turned the bones into the University of Fairbanks. Never will I do that again. I was told this, however, the bones were that of a cave bear and carbon-dated to be 20,000,000 years old.

Rena said at the time of the dig, "Get on with it. We do not have time for this."

Quite so, Rena, quite so. This reminds me of some gold deposits I come across in my treks about Ose Mountain. If I wanted to become rich digging gold, the house would never have been built.

Yes, there is gold near Ose Mountain, but the real gold is the castle Rena and I built.

Rena, my queen. All the gold in the world can never replace you.

Love, Duane

CHAPTER 14

Some Say I Wished, We Say Did

After the basement walls were in place, the outsides of them were also treated and covered by forty-pound felt, plus black poly sheeting to ensure a vapor barrier and dry logs walls. Then back filled.

The plank wood basement flooring was on raised girders mitered into the posts, with floor joists between them. Again, no wood ever touched the volcanic ash. On the ash under the wood, there is a two-inch space minimum now between poly sheeting for a ground vapor barrier and the wood, for dryness and to stop dust.

At that point, winter had set in, and nothing more could be done as far as outside work. We became snowbirds and spent the winter with Mom on the Ose farm in Minnesota. The next spring, we were back at it.

I tilled a large garden, and Rena was happy. Everything grew. So much so that we fed the people of Nenana; we had so much.

Over the nine years of living in the dugout, we moved into the three-story log castle. We had help from God, good friends, relatives, and a young East German man that served in that army. Three men from Norway, two from Minnesota, one was my son Dan. Owen and Eric Ose, cousins from Arizona. A very hard worker from Alabama came every winter in his off time.

Thank you, Trond Paterson, for helping me build the 16×36-foot greenhouse and nearly sawing off my thumb; the scar remains. Fun times.

Thank you, Owen, for helping me bring that 58-foot log up three miles and place it on the house. It only took us two days.

Thank you, Dan, for hiking in the 57 miles to find the land on which to build Ose Mountain.

Book 1

Thank you, Jeff Peterson, for your help cutting the 3.5-mile trail, building the outhouse and dugout.

Book 2

Thank you, Larry Braw (Browser).

Book 3

Thank you, Chad K. The survivor of me falling an 80-foot spruce tree on you.

Thank you, Heart-mot-hanker. Thank you, Baby (our pine squirrel).

Take care of the house, Jake the Raven.

Take care of the field mice and rabbits, Hooty the Owl.

Hey, Lynx-ey, say hi to the rest of the Lynx

Hello to the Alaskan wildfire crews.

Yupper, Rena and I had over thirty some years of happy life on Ose Mountain.

God bless you, my Queen Rena. I shall be walking with you hand in hand again someday.

Our Ose legacy, Rena, will go on no matter what some Brit sheep farmers say. There was a good reason the first shot was fired in 1776.

Each nation shall be a sovereign country on to itself.

Live on. "The Rising of the Phoenix."

Thank you, Eric, for you and Rena in raising the two massive A-frames for the 16-foot cathedral ceiling. For the three bedrooms.

After supper and things to do around the house, I took that time to make the runway. That took me three summers to complete. The castle only took six cords of heating wood. Most times, I alone cut stacked that during the month of September.

We had a 100-mile trap line. Rena, being an expert sewer, also became an expert skinner. Her craftsmanship was in demand by the world buyers. Because of her art of doing all the fur taxidermy, Rena gets the credit for bringing home the bacon. Thank you, Queen Rena. I only did the easy part.

Rena, while helping me build a wood fence around the first small garden, broke her ankle and had to be flown out.

While living in the new log house at one point, I had a sleepless agonizing night. In the morning Rena was flown to the Fairbanks Hospital. After she woke up in the recovery room and I at her side, she was told by the surgeon, "You, young lady, had a heart attack and now have two stents."

Please Google the next for an excellent TV interview and thank you: Ose Mountain the Last Homesteader of Alaska KSTP TV

Rena and I gave our land, home, tools, two ATVs, two 660-cc wide track Artic Cat snowmobiles. All toll land, house, etc., worth $1,000,000. Even more, our over thirty years of love, sweat, and tears of joy to a so-called reality show in the 2-4 CO-UK. Three companies are making $000,000, and Rena and I were burned and taken. Rena and I had no thoughts of being used.

Regardless of what is said or read, we got after taxes perhaps enough to pay for a half of a new small car. Plus no royalties or gratuities of the six-hour series. We were paid a gainful employment taxable income by BBC UK. All we got was notoriety.

The highly viewed on two well-known media is called "Win the Wilderness Alaska."

The British couple that won are unmarried English sheep farmers and have washed their hands of Ose Mountain. But they have not given it back to me at the time of this writing yet to be published on September 18, 2021, and are only continuing to make money from there blogs of Ose Mountain. Ose Mountain sits vacant. My heart is on Ose Mountain and not too far from now, my ashes too.

I pray that the Brits stop playing me for a sap and return to me Ose Mountain with no strings attached. Else it will be 1776 all over again.

I and Rena, the king and queen of Ose Mountain, want this to be known throughout the world that smoking kills. Rena had stopped smoking five years prior to her death. But the damage was done. As king, I believe in the freedom of choice. But I say to you, choose wisely.

Rena had an open-heart surgery and did not recover. Her two choices were to risk dying in surgery or bleeding out anywhere at any time. She was very brave and chose to have the operation. She went out the door, kissing our goodbyes like she was only to have an oil change on the car and would be right back.

I should have seen more intuitive when she told me where in the cupboards we had the food stuffs. Rena was a brave woman and saw to it that certain things were given away to her good friends. Wills, life insurance, to even paying first for her funeral, then mine as well.

Rena did all this so matter-of-factly that all fears were set aside.

It was time.

While lying on the operating table with her head slightly raised, looking at the team of six surgeons, Rena's last words were and in her typical humorous self said these words, "Well! Are we going to do this or not? Let's get on with it."

This is what the main surgeon told me. He went on to say that this was the longest surgery he ever had. What typically lasted six hours was thirteen hours. The tearing of the flesh about the arteries and the mending of with the blood transfusions. The team could not keep up.

Rena was a fighter to the end. Her death was pronounced at 6:37 p.m. on May14, 2021.

I was called and told on the phone of her passing. (The days when no one was allowed in the hospitals but personnel and patients.)

When I arrived, now standing by her side, she looked like she did when fast asleep aside me in bed.

I kissed her on the lips, held her hand, talked to her, and confessed my love. Then as we always did each day, I said to her, this time my last good night.

The leaving of our castle was too much for her and me. The stress weighed heavy on us, as I too, after leaving our wilderness home of thirty-plus years, had a heart attack. Like Rena, I too now have two stents. Rena made a comment about that.

"He had to catch up with me and have two stents too and laughs."

But no worries, Rena, our legacy of Ose Mountain will live on. After I die, my ashes will be on Ose Mountain too, blended in with yours, Queen Rena. Together, we will be in heaven.

I miss you, Rena.

Love, Your King Duane.

Love is never ending.

Lightning Source UK Ltd.
Milton Keynes UK
UKHW020728090223
416597UK00011B/441